# Go In and In:

## Poems from the Heart of Yoga

By
Danna Faulds

Peaceable Kingdom Books
Greenville, Virginia

ISBN 978-0-9744106-0-9

Cover Photograph Copyright © 1997 by Morris Press

Copies of this book along with
Danna's second book of poetry titled:
*One Soul: More Poems From the Heart of Yoga*
are available by mail.
Send $15.00 (includes shipping) to:
Danna Faulds
53 Penny Lane
Greenville VA 24440
The author may be e-mailed at:
yogapoems@aol.com

Printed in the U.S.A. by
Morris Publishing
3212 East Highway 30
Kearney, NE 68847
1-800-650-7888

## Dedication

To Richard, my husband and my love.

You saw who I really was long before I did, and inspired my first tentative steps in the direction of this book. Your patient, and loving support uplifted me, made me laugh, kept me grounded in reality and helped me learn to say yes. Thank you for listening with such love, and for being a true partner on our shared path of awakening. It doesn't get any better than this!

# Contents

Introduction.....................................................................

Acknowledgements.......................................................x

Gifts of Practice..........................................................

Gifts of Life............................................................... 2

Gifts of Nature.......................................................... 5

Gifts of Union.......................................................... 7

Index of Titles and First Lines................................... 9

# Introduction

It was May, 1990 when I had the good fortune to take part in a day-long retreat for staff at Kripalu Center. One segment of the retreat involved a series of meditation experiences, followed by an automatic writing exercise. We were instructed to write the words "This is what I have to say to you" at the top of a sheet of blank paper, and then just write whatever came – no editing, no worrying about word choice, no stopping to think what came next. Just write. A bit skeptical, I did what I was told.

*This is what I have to say to you. You forget over and over who you are. You think you are a small self locked in a body - nothing more than your personal collection of weaknesses and fears. When you forget, the loneliness and fear become overwhelming and nothing you do is enough to break through the wall of your self rejection.*

*To hate yourself is, quite simply, to hate God. For it is God clothed in a body, that you are. To doubt yourself, to feel loathsome, to see nothing but imperfection and failure - these things are only possible because you have forgotten the truth of who you are. Perfection is neither necessary nor possible, but remembrance goes a long way toward making the journey a joyful one. I tell you that in the end, reunion is assured...*

Reading over what I had written, I took in a message perfectly tailored to my needs, was touched by the kindness of the writter "voice," and amazed by the fact that I had written something from the deepest core of my being. On some level, I knew what I wrote was true. The retreat continued on to the next thing, but often during that day and the days that followed, I reflected on the power and simplicity of that writing.

Could I write like that on my own? Could I write withou a long period of meditation, and without the energy of a group t carry me forward? Could I just pick up a pen and find that there was, indeed, something that I had to say to myself?

A few days after the retreat I grabbed a pen and paper, and climbed to the apple orchard behind Kripalu. Picking just the right tree, I made myself comfortable, leaning back against the trunk, a view of blue sky showing through the apple blossoms. Nervous, I took a few deep breaths and wrote at the top of the page "This is what I have to say to you." On cue, I found my mind flooded with words that vied for space on the page as my pen raced to keep up.

*This is what I have to say to you. You know all that you need to know. You already are all that you need to be. It remains only for you to recognize and acknowledge who you are, what you know, and the powerful presence that is awake within you. You think of yourself as fragile, but you are, in fact, strong. You sometimes feel alone, but you are, in truth, connected through Spirit to all beings. The power of God works through you, making all things possible. Believe in this connection. Believe yourself. That is all you need to do, for all is well.*

This voice, wherever it came from, definitely had my number. The words spoke to the essence of the doubts that assailed me day to day. When I walked down the hill from the orchard that evening, I suspected that writing might hold a key to self-understanding and acceptance that had eluded me despite efforts to address those doubts through meditation, yoga and other spiritual practices.

I gradually integrated a daily experience of "free writing" into my practice time. Each morning, during the flow of movement, breath, and meditation that is Kripalu Yoga, I would pick up my journal and write the words "This is what I have to say to you," then let the words flow in any direction that they chose. To my surprise, I was never at a loss for something to say. Whenever I picked up the pen, there was a message to be written – some gift, however small, from the quiet voice within.

I found that if I surrendered to the experience and allowed words to come through me rather than trying to force or create them, wisdom, humor and lightness were nearly always available. These daily messages changed in response to life circumstances, but the easy, supportive tone remained consistent no matter what challenges I might be facing.

Experimenting, I found that I could write any time I decided to stop for a moment, pick up a pen, take a few deep breaths, and let myself be open to the flow of words. I could write in the middle of a hectic day at work or before falling into an exhausted sleep at night. I could write in the midst of a migraine, or in the hospital a day after having major surgery. There was no limit to the accessibility of the inner voice.

I found that hearing exactly what I needed to know, understanding where and why I was blocked or stumbling, didn't necessarily translate into easy or practical life solutions. Sometimes I'd remain stuck in old habit patterns and belief systems despite having articulated exactly what I needed to gain freedom. I could write about inviting peace into my conscious awareness in the morning, and never think another peaceful thought in the midst of a particularly hectic day. I might write "Let not your heart be troubled" at 7:00 A.M. and follow it with a day of worry, self judgment or interpersonal conflict.

Yet, slowly, undeniably, I allowed what I wrote to have an impact on my life. While transformation has its own timetable and will not be hurried along, I found myself accepting how I showed up in life and bypassing my usual pattern of self-rejection. I discovered a sense of spaciousness to life that I could date back to the beginning of a regular writing practice. And even when I found myself in the depths of self-loathing once again, I didn't choose to remain there for long.

Despite the disconnect between my writing and ability to practice, significant changes began to flow from my writing into my life. As I wrote about trusting myself, putting aside harsh self-judgments, accepting and even celebrating life's very human struggles, I slowly but surely began to change.

I don't think any of us pass through childhood unscathed. I certainly didn't. Despite my parents' best intentions, I arrived at adulthood with an abiding belief in my own unworthiness, and a mind that threw doubt, fear, and self-judgment in my face at the slightest provocation. I was often my own worst enemy. Writing afforded me an opportunity to hear what I needed to hear. Every day I had a dependable, accessible source of wisdom, truth and affirmation with which to counter the voice of fear or doubt. Writing fostered a level of self-trust, faith and independence that enhanced my day-to-day experience of life.

I have dealt with depression all my life, beginning in childhood when it was passed off as moodiness. Every so often, defying rational explanation, I'd spiral down and get lost inside myself. Writing gave me an avenue of expression when I was so depressed that it was hard to get words out of my mouth. It helped me hold the experience of despair more lightly, bringing a glimmer of light into the darkness of the psyche. Writing afforded me a foothold in what otherwise felt like a formless, slippery pit, a way of contacting who and what I really was underneath or behind the mask of emptiness that depression molded on the features of my face.

Nearly two years after the retreat in which I had my first experience with this kind of writing, there was a significant shift in what flowed from my pen. Unbidden, and completely unexpected, I found myself writing a poem. I was stunned, not so much by the content of the poem, as by the change in form. The page before me held these words:

*Lord, lead me to the song of my heart*
*and help me sing it unashamed.*

*Help me to stand before you in bare consciousness,*
*unflinching in your light.*

*Lead me to the expression of my soul*
*in all its fullness.*

*Let me embrace my humanity,*
*yet be anchored in divinity.*

*Help me unfetter the joy that I am.*

*Lead me to the stillness of my soul*
*where love and union dwell as one.*

*May I uplift others in the recognition*
*of their magnificence.*

*May I see the vastness of my own soul,*
*and embrace it, unafraid and whole.*

The words captured a longing in my heart that I had nev before expressed on paper. This was my soul speaking with its creator. The words came with no effort or foreknowledge. I didn't sit, pen in hand, with the intention of writing a poem. M experience was that I picked up the pen the way I did every morning, and instead of prose, there was a poem.

After that day, poetry began to replace prose, slowly at first, and then with more frequency. Some days the poems would be skeletal and halting. Other days an entire poem would pour forth in need of only minor editorial changes. There was a lyrical quality to these poems, a rhyme and meter that carried the message of the day more gracefully than prose. The addition of poetry strengthened my commitment to writing as a spiritual practice.

Writing became my way of accessing the spark of the divine that I believe resides within each one of us. That spark, with its wisdom, energy and truth, was always within reach. It was the fuel for poems, life decisions, consciousness, and being fully alive.

Did all this require a huge time commitment on my part? No way. I worked full-time for much of the last twelve years as my writing matured, changed, and turned in the direction of poetry. I rarely had more than a few minutes each morning to write the words, "This is what I have to say to you," and send myself off into a busy day on a foundation of assurance and truth. Ten minutes was enough to catch the drift of a poem that I would later edit to completion. I would pick up my pen and see what came. I'd follow the thread of words to its simple conclusion, then go on my way.

In 1996 I wrote these words:

*I write myself into being.*
*From the stillness,*
*day by day*
*the words arise,*
*and who I am*
*appears on paper...*

I have written myself into a willingness to embrace polarity, ambiguity, sorrow, suffering and joy. I have written when depression dragged me so deeply into myself I felt I would never again escape the bleak and formless landscape of despair. I have written to describe peak experiences, awareness and the choices and cares that make up life. Truly, I have written the person I now know as myself into being.

These days, I choose to spend more time on writing. Some mornings I begin my day with the words "This is what I have to say to you," and let the prose flow, but it is poetry that most often calls to me now. Poetry is a paradox. On the one hand each poem is a gift, taking shape in emptiness, and manifesting on the page when I manage to get out of the way. On the other hand, poetry is definitely work, albeit a labor of love.

This book is a collection of my favorite poems written over the last six years. It is divided into four sections: "the gifts of practice" - poems touching on or arising from yoga, meditation, and other spiritual practices; "the gifts of life" which arose from my experience of being human and dealing with everything from fear and doubt to relationship. There are "the gifts of nature," poems inspired by the natural world, and "the gifts of union" which had their genesis in moments of realization, expanded awareness or awakening. It is in these concluding poems that the voice of spirit expresses most freely.

I offer these poems to you, completing a circle; sharing what I've received and what has been meaningful to me. Each poem has played a role in my life journey. I wrote them for myself; they spoke the words I needed to hear at the time. If they also speak to you, that will be yet another gift to me. If they can ease some suffering, bring light where there is shadow, or otherwise help you on your journey, all I can say is "thank you" to the voice that spoke them into being.

In the end, poetry, like life, is a mystery. All I can do is be open and drink freely from its depths, letting my heart be touched and accepting the gifts that flow from a place I cannot see or understand. Offering these poems to you is my way of saying "yes" to the mystery of my life, and acknowledging our connection, you and I, even if we've never met.

And now I'll let the poems speak for themselves.

Danna Spitzform Faulds
June, 2002

# Acknowledgements

I can't pass up this opportunity to thank a number of people for their contributions to this book and to my life. First, I would like to thank Sudhir Jonathan Foust, President of Kripalu Center. Back in 1990 he was a program teacher, and it was he who led the retreat experience in which I first began writing. Sudhir, who would have believed that your skillful suggestion to write, "This is what I have to say to you" would lead to this book?

My dear husband Richard heard every one of these poems, usually on the day it was written. His willingness to support me while I wrote, along with his insightful comments and unconditional love helped bring this book to fruition.

Thanks to my family: my father Hal Spitzform, who bought me anthologies of poetry even when he didn't care much for poetry himself; my sister Marianne Spitzform who encouraged me with frequent e-mails and understood what it meant to break out of a small, secure life; my brother Peter Spitzform who loved me from the day he was born, cheered me on, led me to believe that my writing was worthwhile, and made me laugh when I took myself too seriously; and to my mother, Mary Spitzform, who died nearly ten years ago. She trusted my ability to write long before I did, and her presence in my life is dearly and daily missed.

I thank all the participants of the noon yoga class I taught at Kripalu, my first public audience for these poems. I have been enriched by every yoga student, and each participant in a program, workshop or conference in which I've read my poetry. Thank you for listening deeply and receiving me with such openness.

To Yogi Amrit Desai and the entire Kripalu community, I extend my gratitude for teaching by example and experience that the path of transformation passes through the flames.

Special thanks to Paul Weiss, whose mastery of the Enlightenment Intensive process launched my writing on a new trajectory, and to his compatriots in consciousness, Barbara Mary Thomas and Bettina Dudley.

Len and Ling Ming Poliandro showed me what friendship, creativity and courage were all about, and inspired poems with their artwork.

Marc and Meryl Rudin opened their hearts, their home, and their chiropractic office for impromptu poetry readings and the deep discussion of things that really matter.

Guy Kettelhack's fearless pursuit of truth in his writing, artwork, and a stream of e-mails stretching across miles and decades provided encouragement when it was most needed.

To all the friends who have supported me, listened to my poems, made suggestions, and loved me through the fear and doubt that accompanied writing poetry and reading it in public: Stephen Cope, Bhaskar Deva, Nischala Devi, Carol Edwards,

John and Kay Faulds, Suzanne Selby Grenager, Felicity Hood, Bill Hydon, Sneha Karen Jegart, Dan Jones, Margaret and Lloyd Klapperich, Kathy Kuser, Sudha Carolyn Lundeen, Andrea Mather, Al Meyerer, Lawrence Noyes, Jeffrey Reel, Bruce Storms, Paul Striberry, Kathryn and Peter Tausig, and Earnestine Woodliff.

And to Marc Paul Volavka, I send my love and gratitude for the redemptive power of forgiveness and the choice to build bridges.

# The

# Gifts

# Of

# Practice

Go in and in.
   Be the space
between two cells,
   the vast, resounding
silence in which
   spirit dwells.
Be sugar dissolving
   on the tongue of life.
Dive in and in,
   as deep as you can dive.
Be infinite, ecstatic truth.
   Be love conceived and born in union.
Be exactly what you seek,
   the Beloved, singing Yes,
tasting Yes, embracing Yes,
   until there is only essence;
the All of Everything
   expressing through you
as you. Go in and in
   and turn away from
nothing that you find.

## The Weaver and the Loom

Sit here for a bit.  Place yourself
outside the frenzied pace of life.
Slow down long enough to
appreciate birds in flight, water
drops like prisms in the grass and
countless shades of green.  Step
off the fast track and listen to the
sound of breath and birdsong.  Take
a moment to just be, and in the being,
know the whole of this creation,
mystery and madness, passion and
profanity, know it all as one, stunning
tapestry.  Sit still and the thin line
between sacred and profane simply
fades away.  There is nothing then
to reconcile.  All the disparate threads
are woven on the loom of life.  Sit here
for a bit and your unique place in the
pattern becomes clear.  Take the still
point with you when it's time to walk
away.  Make the choice to see affinity,
to watch the picture taking shape as
thread joins thread.  Dare to be the
weaver and the loom, creator and
creation, the sower and the sown.
In a moment of stillness, all that
came before is seen as one.

3

# Breath

Breath, the mindful breath,
the rhythm, out and in,
the wave that washes
through our days, creating
space for stillness, sorrow,
joy, or exaltation.  Full,
then empty, ebb and flow,
breath accompanies each
step into the unknown.
In the breath, the soul
finds an opportunity to
speak. Images or intuition,
poetry or wordless wisdom
come and go -- no effort but
to breathe and listen.

Do yoga with no goal but
to be in the moment.  This
breath, this stretch, this wave
of emotion rolling in.  Watch it
crest, and break, then dissipate.

Hold the body like a
lover in a close embrace,
listening with intimacy,
touching with tenderness.

Yoga is a threshold into
mystery; each pose an
open doorway and an
invitation to unfold.

Sensations rise and fall,
and through it all the
deathless center radiates
the simple truth of union.

## Being Present

Breathe, relax and feel;
take time to slow down
the pace of life.  Watch the
rise and fall of moods, the
birth and death of dreams.
Feelings and sensations seem
so real, yet they shift like
changing clouds, and flow
with the high tide out to sea
again.  Allow it all to be, no
need to grasp or push away.
Present with each moment,
the whole of you, body, mind
and soul, opens to receive.

## Witness

When I can be the witness,
all manner of miracles occur –
old wounds heal, the past
reveals itself to be released,
present dramas play themselves
out without sinking emotional
talons into my soft skin. The
witness welcomes truth and
dares to meet reality on its
own terms. It is the ground
in which the seeds of
transformation take root
and finally flower. When
the witness is awake, the
lake of mind is still, and
in that mirrored surface,
I see my own true face as
Spirit smiling back at me.

## Meditation

A touch, like the whisper
of a wing feather at the
top of the head.  There is
a hint of energy moving,
and closed eyes rise to
follow.  This is such a
subtle shift, easy to miss,
simpler to say it's just a
current of air, but no, the
upward pull will not be
denied.  There is within
a caged bird longing to
fly, a spark that knows it's
part of a sacred fire, a soul
that yearns for home and
freedom, and senses the
infinite possibility of both
in moments like this when
a golden silence holds the
whole world in its thrall,
the only sound the rise
and fall of breath.

## Still Point

There is a quality of
stillness so rare that
the air shimmers in its
presence.  It's there
between our eyes.
We hear it when we
dare to speak the truth.
It vibrates with the
music of life, dances
in the wind, breaks
forth from the trees
into a clearing just
as the sun rises, and
settles into silence
once again.  There is
a quality of stillness
so rare that I am bared
to the vary marrow of
my bones before it.
May I choose never
to be clothed again.

Breath of Life

I breathe in All That Is –
Awareness expanding
to take everything in,
as if my heart beats
the world into being.

From the unnamed
vastness beneath the
mind, I breathe my
way to wholeness
and healing.

Inhalation.  Exhalation.
Each breath a "yes,"
and a letting go,
a journey, and a
coming home.

# Yoga

Yoga is not about the pose.
It's not the alignment of
toes or hips or shoulders.
It's not about the form.

Yoga is an invitation to
explore, not a command
performance.  It speaks
the language of the soul.

In the flow of breath and
motion, yoga coaxes us
from the confines of the
known, across the silent
threshold into vastness.

Yoga is the union of prayer
and movement, guided from
inside.  It is healing and the
joy of saying yes to life.

Breathe, relax and feel the
body receive its own truth.
The seed of freedom flowers
within each of us whenever
we are open to what's real.

## This is Prana

Hands open to receive or
give, and on the surface of
each palm a vortex spins,
a galaxy of light and wind.
Hands lift, arms reach not
to beseech or beg, but
a drifting, dreamy, grateful
movement, leading once
again to stillness.  Hands
grow hot, then cool, and
energy builds, a pool of life
force waits for the shift
from potential to kinetic.
The world spirals into this
slow breath, sensation, the
suspension of time and mind,
love suffusing everything.

# Birthright

Despite illness of body or mind,
in spite of blinding despair or
habitual belief, who you are
is whole.  Let nothing keep you
separate from the truth.  The soul,
illumined from within, longs to
be known for what it is.  Undying,
untouched by fire or the storms of
life, there is a place inside where
stillness and abiding peace reside.
You can ride the breath to go there.
Despite doubt or hopeless turns of
mind, you are not broken.  Spirit
surrounds, embraces, fills you from
the inside out.  Release everything
that isn't your true nature.  What's
left, the fullness, light, and shadow,
claim all that as your birthright.

## Walk Slowly

It only takes a reminder to breathe,
a moment to be still, and just like that,
something in me settles, softens, makes
space for imperfection.  The harsh voice
of judgment drops to a whisper and I
remember again that life isn't a relay
race; that we will all cross the finish
line; that waking up to life is what we
were born for.  As many times as I
forget, catch myself charging forward
without even knowing where I'm going,
that many times I can make the choice
to stop, to breathe, and be, and walk
slowly into the mystery.

## The Soul of Yoga

What is the soul of yoga?
Follow your heart into the
center of the pose and find
in the midst of detail and
precision, in breath, alignment,
balance, bliss, fear and sadness –
at the very core of all of this
is love.  Touch upon your
truest nature even once and
the experience of what you
really are sears the psyche
like the surface of the sun.
The soul of yoga, the gift
within the pose is the
moment of communion,
resting in pure essence,
the awakening as if from
sleep to the face of
unmistakable divinity;
the ineffable wonder and
living reality of spirit – oh,
yes – the soul of yoga is love.

## Slow Motion Prana

Hands lift, float,
drift. No mere dream;
this is life force,
made manifest –
healing held
in the palms
of your two hands.

Let life and prana
lift you to a place
you've never
visited before.

Breath, heart, and
body now aligned,
find the peace
that mind can
only dream of.

## It Doesn't Always
## Smell Like Roses

This body is not flowing
with liquid energy, no,
and this mind is not
awash with peace.  I
fight myself in every
posture, muscles shriek,
fear freezes bone and a
sure sense of failure grows.

This too is practice,
this ground where grief
gains the upper hand,
and anger casts dark
shadows.  This, the flip
side of delight is as much
the point as any pleasure—
this is breathing into life.

# Inner Fire

What does it take to keep the
inner fire of inspiration burning?
What wakes the soul from
sleep when the mind yearns
for any respite from the storm?
What calls forth courage when
fear is a known and frequent
guest?  When the winds of
change and circumstance swirl
in circles, when breath is short
and shallow, what brings release?

The peace of God is present in
the tumult and the temple.
A single thought can move us
from the unreal to the real.
To dance or kneel, to sing or
speak a prayer of gratitude
and praise can spark the flame
of truth again.  To remember
and forget, to find and lose, to
to remember and forget again –
there is no shame in this.

To recall the grace that is
our nature brings down the
wall that separates and draws
the gaze inside once more.
There, the open door of the
heart glows like a beacon
in the night. There, we rest
in stillness and in light.

# The Fruits of Practice

Despite fervent pleas for ease
and safety, there are many days
when reality doesn't quite line
up with what I'd choose.
Breakdown. Letting go.
Surrendering even the illusion
of control. Breathing into the
unknown – sometimes that is
what life holds.

Practice hasn't brought an end
to pain. I still increase my
suffering like a fish caught on
a line. My struggles only draw
the hook in deeper. But being
in reality is its own reward.
It's the perfect paradox; the
courage to stand and breathe
when everything in me wants
to flee is as great a gift as the
freedom to seek retreat.

No, practice hasn't brought
an end to pain but it has honed
my willingness to experience
the moment and sometimes see
perfection unfolding in ways
I wasn't big enough to plan,
much less predict.

Practice isn't about achieving
a goal. It's not a means to pole-
vault over suffering. Practice

is my way of looking life in
the face and saying yes to all
its disparate gifts. Practice
keeps me awake when I would
sleep, and reminds me it's
the journey, unfolding in this
very moment, it's the journey
that reveals the truth, and
not the destination.

# Kripalu

This path, this place, this endeavor
and this day are bigger than our
vision. We are each of us a part
of something vast. We speak
and act, make our way through
moments of despair and showers
of grace. Radiant or bleak, we are
already complete – and there is
still much work to do. Our divine
humanity shows through and we
are humbled, brought to our knees,
raised up again, uplifted and received.
We taste separation and the merging
of souls. This path, this place, this
endeavor and this day have a life of
their own, a mission we can't measure
or contain, a purpose each heart
articulates in different words,
a destiny that will not be denied.
Kripalu, Shiva, Shakti intertwined;
like a phoenix rising scorched and
sacred from the fire, Kripalu is alive.

# I Am All of This

There are as many paths
 to truth as there are
heartbeats, leaves, fireflies
 in summer twilight.  Let me
tell you of the path that's
 chosen me, the road that has
drawn my feet forward,
 the way of my awakening.

Defying easy definition, it
 unfolds, and I follow.  With
each step I let in more of life.
 I expand into vastness.  My
reach exceeds my grasp
 until I hold to nothing solid.

I include, widen, grow deeper.
 This too, is me, and this, and
yes, even this.  There is more
 emptiness than substance here,
and not a single rule to live by.
 In place of form there is an
ecstatic dance with the
 boundless infinity of truth.

There is freedom, stillness,
 song and silence, sustenance
and the end of supplication.
 In place of seeking, there is
finding without loss, and love
 without boundaries.  There
are no walls in this existence.

Here is no difference, out or

in.  All That Is radiates,
quickens, awakens, fills and
        empties in the same breath,
and I know beyond doubt
        or any hesitation, that I am
            all of this.

# The

# Gifts

# of

# Life

## Allow

There is no controlling life.
Try corralling a lightning bolt,
containing a tornado. Dam a
stream, and it will create a new
channel. Resist, and the tide
will sweep you off your feet.
Allow, and grace will carry
you to higher ground. The only
safety lies in letting it all in –
the wild with the weak; fear,
fantasies, failures and success.
When loss rips off the doors of
the heart, or sadness veils your
vision with despair, practice
becomes simply bearing the truth.
In the choice to let go of your
known way of being, the whole
world is revealed to your new eyes.

## Foundation Stones

Here is my past--
what I've been proud of,
and what I've pushed away.
Today I see how each piece
was needed, not a single
step wasted on the way.

Like a stone wall,
every rock resting
on what came before –
no stone can be
suspended in mid-air.

Foundation laid by every
act and omission,
each decision, even
those the mind would
label "big mistake."

The things I thought
were sins, these are as
necessary as successes,
each one resting on the
surface of the last, stone
upon stone, the fit
particular, complete,
the rough, uneven
face of these rocks
makes surprising,
satisfying patterns
in the sunlight.

## Setting Forth

Something will be born from
this goodbye. In the pain of
setting forth, something will
die. With the release of the
old comes a moment when
nothing is firmly held, and
the unknown burns the
bridges of the past.

When the smoke clears, my
eyes seek out the new horizon.
Nothing is known here, but
the air is sweet and breathing
deeply I see long dormant
seeds send up their shoots
from the fertile ground of
change. As leaves unfurl
to meet the sun, the circle
is complete. I will not
forget a single step of this
sacred journey, nor will I
let comfort lock me in its
warm embrace.

I do not know what fruit these
seeds will bear, but I have
faith that what is taking
root today will surprise me
with its vigor. In birth and
death, the inbreath and the
final exhalation, there is
pain and the movement into
truth. I take the step that I
am called to even if I do not
know the final destination.

## Who You Are

Who you are is so much more
than what you do.  The essence,
shining through heart, soul, and
center, the bare and bold truth
of you does not lie in your
to-do list.  You are not just
at the surface of your skin, not
just the impulse to arrange the
muscles of your face into a smile
or a frown, not just boundless
energy, or bone wearying fatigue.
Delve deeper.  You are divinity;
the vast and open sky of Spirit.
It's the light of God, the ember
at your core, the passion and the
presence, the timeless, deathless
essence of you that reaches out
and touches me.  Who you are
transcends fear and turns
suffering into liberation.
Who you are is love.

## Gone Fishing

You seekers of truth,
cast your nets beyond
the mind.  Bait your
lines with longing,
and let love be your
lure.  Watch and wait.
Be patient while your
bobber sits on the
surface and it seems
the expedition is for
naught.  That which
you seek is out of
sight for now.  But
here's the captain's
guarantee – if you can
have no goal but being
one with waves and
sunlight; if you can
welcome equally the
marlin and the minnow,
your catch will be
bigger than your dreams.
When you draw up the
nets and reel in the
lines, your mind will
have to open wide, or
simply stop to receive
such riches as these.

## Enough

It's enough to offer love,
no matter how imperfectly
received or given.  It's
enough to try and fail at
at a difficult task; enough
to fall and rise, stumble,
fall again, sigh, and start
to walk, however slowly,
in the direction the soul
points.  It's enough to
seek peace and find pain,
to gain nothing but a
vision of truth, and take
the long route home.

It's enough to feel
temptation, the dance
of the senses, the hot
pull of desire; enough
to call on God, walk
through fire, sleep and
cry and fear or welcome
dying.  It's enough to be
and breathe, to feel the
touch of wind on skin.

It's enough to take the
day as it comes, to watch
the ripples on the lake as
the rock sinks to the
bottom, to see the wild
reflection of the surface
calm into a mirror once
again.  It's enough to

hear the voice of fear
and hide – or seek it out
and face the shame or
shadows.  It's enough
to set out to tame demons
and watch them multiply
instead.  It's enough to
be buffeted by the winds
of change and not blown
over.  I and you and all
of us, more than enough.

If I knew that
everything I believed
and more was true –
what would I do?  I'd
wake up and let life
take me as its own.
I'd point at fear and
say, "You're not real."
(I'd say this kindly.)
I wouldn't forget that
I am linked to every
flower, fox, fantasy
and planet.  I'd let
love in, and each day
I'd stretch a little more
until I could embrace
the whole horizon.
I'd sip green tea and
savor the taste of
oatmeal raisin cookies.
I'd welcome whatever
came next and know
that the love in your
eyes could change me
forever if I let it.

## Lay the Armor Down

Arriving back from the fields
of battle, bruised and bolder,
we are beholden to no one
now.  Losing or winning –
the reasons for the war fade
quickly in the memory.
We've forgotten that these
suits of armor are not our
second skins.  Smiling, we
set aside the shields and
swords, remove the face
masks, begin to peel away
the layers of weight and
protection.  When, finally,
we cast our armor to the
ground, it feels as if our
bodies grow and straighten,
swell and lengthen upward
toward the sun.  We run,
light and unencumbered,
and stretch the stiffness
from our joints.  Rolling on
the grass we laugh as awkward
limbs remember freedom.
When at last we return to
where we started, without a
second glance we know that
we've outgrown the suits of
armor.  We won't fit inside
those too-tight shells again.
Why would we even try?

Breaking All the Rules

There are moments when rules
are meant to be broken; when
bursting out of context is the
sole way to see with new eyes.
There are fences built only to
be torn down.  The slats look
solid, but no one drove the nails
in tight.  There are barricades
around the heart asking to be
breached.  Sooner or later we
all run out of excuses for
staying small and safe.

## Staring at the Bones

Sooner or later, life in its variety
and wisdom, chews the meat from
the bones of my illusions.  It sucks
the marrow from inside, and throws
the dry bones to bleach in a pile.

Expectations are treated with equal
disdain.  Stripped of their finery, they
are revealed as nothing more than
future plans, easy ways to stay safe,
roadmaps drawn by a blind cartographer
trying to imagine distant destinations.

This is the present moment's boot camp.
Life's lack of rules will be obeyed or I'll
spend my time peeling potatoes in the
past.  I can choose to leave behind the
skeletons of what I thought I knew and
raise the flag of truth on the front porch.

I can take a single step and wait for the
next one to be revealed.  I can only
know where I am in this moment.
Anything else is a desperate attempt
to clothe the bones and set them walking.

## Bull's Eye

This arrow of life
has a trajectory so true
that the center of my heart
is pierced before I feel the pain.
I, who began by seeking myself,
was led by love to you.

Still Life With Fruit

Life will not be neatly
wrapped and tied, boxed
or pigeon-holed.  Just when
we think all the fruit is in
the bowl and we can name
it piece by piece, the still
life is upended.  Plums and
peaches roll to the far corners
of the room.  Now it's the
empty bowl that beckons.
Can we have faith and wait?
Can we allow the mystery of
choice or chance or circumstance
to give birth to fullness once
again?  Can we trust the fruit
will be ripe for picking when
it's time to break the fast?

# The Choice

Is it faith or fear
that rises to the fore,
affirmation or negation
at the very core
and center of the self?

Will it be light or dark
within the heart today?
The icy grip of fear
that knots and sours
leaving me to cower
in the shadows?

There is another way –
I know it surely as I
know the scent of Spring.
The choice of faith
invites, invokes, calls forth
from all creation
both the blessing
and the lesson
of the day.

Whether faith or fear,
the choice is mine alone.
Each moment, choosing,
stepping through the door,
trusting that the path
beyond will surely
lead me home.

## Willingness

In the willingness to feel,
there is healing.  In the
choice not to closet, cast
aside or deny experience,
energy is freed, and I
dive deeper into life.

There may be maturity in
choosing not to act, but
there are no rewards for
suppression and denial.

To be fully alive is saying
yes to the wide array of
human feelings.  When I
soften, release and breathe,
I discover I am more than
what I think, feel, reason,
or believe.

## Surely This is Love

I am intimately connected
with all that is.  When you
water your roots, my heart
blossoms.  When I see you
smile, that's when I know
I'm fully alive.  As you are
able to live in truth, I raise
the roof on this house I am
exploring.  I throw the doors
wide, let the breeze blow in
the windows.  When you
grow, I know it as my own
opening.  You stretch, I
breathe.  I give, and you
receive.  Just beneath the
fabric of our lives, coiled,
ready to spring or budding
like a rose, reaching out to
embrace, or sitting, bathed
in grace and stillness –
this singing, circling, radiant,
one with everything – surely
this is love.

## Embodied Spirit

I am embodied.
Currents of desire
follow your fingers
as they trace soft
circles on my skin.

Embodied, I eat and
sweat, and swear.
I let bare flesh taste
summer sun, and run
through fields of high
grass, laughing
when I stumble.

I am embodied.
Senses are seldom fully
sated.  I long to make
music; listen to bullfrogs;
lie with glistening skin
after we have fully loved;
taste the first sweet
strawberries of
summer; find Jupiter's
moons, and gaze
at the Milky Way
until star depths
leave me dizzy.

I am embodied,
and this is no mistake.

When the sun rises in the heart,
the only response to life, shouted,
sung or whispered, the bridge
between what came before and
now, the single, simple answer
to all prayers, the life-changing
voice of spirit says with certainty
and strength a resounding, clear,
unequivocal "Yes!" to all that is.

## Together

We call down grace,
and gaze without wavering
into the fires of creation.

We find the place where
love embraces fear, and
tears taste like faith.

We let our radiance
be revealed in laughter
and in longing.

We hold the whole of life,
sweet grapes and bitter,
healing herbs -

We hold until we overflow
and offer back the gifts
that we've received.

The vessel never empties.
The growing love between
us keeps it filled.

Life comes as is - no warranties,
no extra button sewn inside the
sleeve, no spare tire in the trunk.
The twists and turns of circumstance
or illness catch us unaware, each
day a thousand reasons to despair,
lament, forget the reason we are
here. And yet, despite the odds,
the flame inside each one of us
burns true. Like butterflies
emerging from cocoons, we
learn to spread our wings and
fly. We seek and find the light.

This body/mind is born with all
that is required to know freedom.
Over time, we find life's only
guarantee -- we cannot be
separated from divinity, nor
cut off from the source of our
supply. Yes, we will age and
die, yet that is but a change in
form. The essence of us soars
as freely as a butterfly over
fields of wildflowers. Beauty
sipping nectar, blessed and
evanescent. In form and
essence, we are beauty,
whole and simply present.

## Paradox

Fear and love seldom
stand, shoulder to shoulder;
It's rare to laugh and
lie in the same breath.

But strength and weakness,
failure and success,
faith and desolation –
they are different ends
of a single stick.

To pick one up
is to receive both poles –
stark contrasts contribute
to a knowledge of the whole.

What is life but growing
wide and deep, so
open from weeping
that opposites, ambiguity,
and a thousand shades
of gray can co-exist
without despair?

A life of truth walks the edge
between ease and effort.
There's nothing you must do
to win approval, no list of
saintly acts to tick off one by one,
no required deprivations. Say yes
to life and you are blessed with
countless opportunities to choose
wholeness over fragmentation.
You need but knock for doors
to open wide. Ask and you are
filled with a presence so vast
that all the words in your
personal lexicon amount to
nothing in its silence. Stop
seeking long enough to
receive the spirit that's within
you now. Just be your truest
self, and the voice you've
longed to hear will speak
through you. Release your
grip on limitation and
possibilities roll out like
endless ocean waves. All
you have to do is kick off
your shoes and run barefoot
in the sand.

Pilgrims on the Path of Love

(For Tom Gillis)


Life spirals in until it is a single point of light –
the soul, in all its radiance, glowing. Control is
not easily relinquished, as we watch the sum
and substance of our days diminishing.  The
breath itself becomes a prayer for sustenance,
for the strength to bear whatever comes.
When two hearts share from the very
center of the sacred, when the
surface of  things is stripped
clean, we are swept away
like leaves floating on
an Autumn stream,
each one a pilgrim
on the path of
love.

## Let It Go

Let go of the ways you thought life
would unfold; the holding of plans
or dreams or expectations – Let it
all go.  Save your strength to swim
with the tide.  The choice to fight
what is here before you now will
only result in struggle, fear, and
desperate attempts to flee from the
very energy you long for.  Let go.
Let it all go and flow with the grace
that washes through your days whether
you receive it gently or with all your
quills raised to defend against invaders.
Take this on faith: the mind may never
find the explanations that it seeks, but
you will move forward nonetheless.
Let go, and the wave's crest will carry
you to unknown shores, beyond your
wildest dreams or destinations. Let it
all go and find the place of rest and
peace, and certain transformation.

## Sangha

Teach me what I cannot learn alone.
Let us share what we know, and what
we cannot fathom.  Speak to me of
mysteries, and let us never lie
to one another.

May our fierce and tender longing
fuel the fire in our souls.  When we
stand side by side, let us dare to focus
our desire on the truth.  May we be
reminders, each for the other, that
the path of transformation passes
through the flames.

To take one step is courageous;
to stay on the path day after day,
choosing the unknown, and facing
yet another fear, that is nothing
short of grace.

## Healing

There is healing in the laying on of hands;
in the letting go of fear, in asking for help,
in silence, celebration, prayer. There is
healing in speaking the truth and in keeping
still, in seeking sunlight and not shunning
struggle. Laughter and the affirmation of
wholeness hold their own healing. When
the soul dances, when the day begins in
delight, when love grows and cannot be
contained, when life flows from moment
to moment, healing happens in the space
between thoughts, and the breath before
the first sung note. Healing is a birthright
and a grace. When we dare to be open to
the unknown, when we extend ourselves
in caring, when we welcome in the vast
expanse of life, healing comes from the
heart, and blossoms from the inside out.

Something in me is being pulled
out at the roots, thrashed on the
ground, the tender parts bared,
beaten, left to dry and blow away
like so much chaff.  Something is
dying.  The clear sky of mind is
obscured by cloud and illusion.
The moon neither rises nor sets
now, and the debts of a lifetime
demand payment.  This is when
faith is tested.  The choice to
discredit what I know and
crawl into a hole of my own
making will leave me bereft
of any consolation.  To be
present in pain is the only path
worth taking.  To acknowledge
light is not denying darkness,
but oh, how hard it is to recall
there is a choice, a chance to ask
for strength and grace.  And in
the asking, there is the subtlest
of shifts, an opening, nearly
imperceptible; an opening to
receive.  There is one ray of
light, then more.  I open the
door, take one deep breath,
and begin another day.

## Awakening Now

Why wait for your awakening?
The moment your eyes are open,
seize the day. Would you hold
back when the Beloved beckons?
Would you deliver your litany
of sins like a child's collection
of sea shells, prized and labeled?
"No, I can't step across the
threshold," you say, eyes
downcast. "I'm not worthy.
I'm afraid, and my motives
aren't pure. I'm not perfect,
and surely I haven't practiced
nearly enough. My meditation
isn't deep, and my prayers are
sometimes insincere. I still chew
my fingernails, and the refrigerator
isn't clean." Do you value your
reasons for staying small more
than the light shining through
the open door? Forgive yourself.
Now is the only time you have
to be whole. Now is the sole
moment that exists to live in
the light of your true Self.
Perfection is not a prerequisite
for anything but pain. Please,
oh please, don't continue to
believe in your disbelief. This
is the day of your awakening.

# The

# Gifts

# of

# Nature

# Nothing is Impossible

I tell you, this was no
    ordinary rainbow.
It stretched low and wide,
    the spectrum reaching
inside the mountain, tickling
    the tops of trees with
    indigo and red.
I gaped and laughed and leaped.
    I tell you, it was something,
this rainbow, and I took it
    for a sign.
"A sign of what?" you ask.
    "That nothing is impossible,"
I answer.  That gladiolas
    can shoot up through a blue
Persian rug; that the
    stars in Orion's belt can join
a rhythm and blues band;
    that squirrels can count change
at the basketball game;
    and grapefruits as bit as bowling
balls can roll into the
    kitchen in time for tomorrow's
breakfast.  I tell you, this
    was no run of the mill rainbow.
The arc is with me still,
    its promise steering me clear
of whatever passes
    for normality around here.

## Single-Celled Elegance

Successful microbes mutate.
They see an evolutionary need,
become the seed that spawns a
different being.  They seize
chance opportunities, try new
paths, have no fear of changing
appearances.  These single cells
hold the keys to transformation.
They equate stagnation with death
and see that releasing form is the
only way to enter into essence.

Here is a day,
dawn to dark,
a string of moments
small enough to
ignore or notice,
a stretch of time
between awakening
and sleep to be
savored, or brushed
aside in the rush
to some distant
destination. Here
is a day, different
from any other,
with its own flavor
to be tasted. The
golden glow just
before the sun
rose held such
promises as I
knew must be kept –
knew beyond even
the nagging whisper
of doubt were true –
that this very day
the whole perfection
of the universe can
be inhaled like the
scent of fallen leaves,
the heady fragrance
of trees returning what
was never theirs to keep.

## Spider Webs

The ragged remnants of
    webs weave like
drunken dreams in the
    spaces between fence
posts and slats,
    fraying in the fall breeze.
One web, its summer
    perfect symmetry
outlined in dew and
    sunshine, silent testimonial
to what was caught
    and killed, eaten and
digested in a season of
    spidering here on the back
deck.  One small, irregular
    hole speaks of struggle,
maybe even release,
    but there is no record save
my own flight of fantasy,
    no minstrel to sing of
heroic feats, of spiders
    slain, moths freed to
circle the porch lights
    that night, sure they had
been reborn to find the
    answers to all mysteries.

## Black-Eyed Susans

It's all here in this single
stalk of black-eyed susans,
two dozen small suns,
rising on a single stem.
It's all here, the whole
season of rain and dry
days, a summer of
sunlight, the waxing and
the waning moon, crickets,
spiders, and butterflies
with stained glass wings.
It's all here, buds and
roots drawing earthblood
up through stalk and shoots,
each blossom a universe,
no galaxy greater than the
ring of golden petals joined
at the dark center.
Answers not found in the
fresh faces of the flowers
are simply not worth seeking.

## Grayson Highlands

Emerging from the darkness of the tent
into shimmering starlight,
we stand transfixed and speechless.
Even the crickets are quiet before this spectacle.
Orion reclines on the horizon,
and nameless constellations in plenty
march across the sky.
Shooting stars disappear before the eye
can turn to fully see them.

In the cool night air, pungent with pine,
there is only dark and stars,
the countless stars,
the shocking breadth and depth
and stillness of stars.
We inhale stars and exhale stars,
a whirling galaxy of stars,
until the nighthawk calls us home.

Waiting For Safety

Fern,
furled,
a question mark
waving in the wind,
holding to the fetal curl
and the safety
of the winter womb.

Nothing,
not the gentle
kiss of sun,
nor stream voice,
calling,
can coax
that frond
to unfurl
one single moment
before it does.

## Estuary

There is peace here, where the river
widens to meet the sea. The rapids
are past; the boulders and the rocky
places at last give way to a broad
and sweeping current, flowing
slowly into vastness. The river
moves silently, tastes the salty tide
that marks its demise, and slips
without a backward glance, into
the ocean's infinite embrace.

## Ocracoke Island

Overnight, each piece
of dune grass
traced a perfect
semicircle
in the sand.
We worship at the
altar of the dunes,
the sunrise
our sanctuary candle,
the hiss and roar
of the breakers,
sacred music,
the swirl of water
around our ankles,
slipping over our feet
like silk,
is our communion.

## Loss of Innocence

A chickadee flew off
the feeder.  You know
chickadees – flying
balls of energy and
attitude.  This one
flew full tilt into
a piece of reflected
sky.  I heard the
thud as bird hit
glass, saw it flutter,
stunned, barely
aloft, watched it land
on the deck railing
not a foot from
where I sat.  His
beak was open,
gasping, eyes
blinking rapidly
as if to clear his
vision of a memory
he preferred to forget.
The small breast
heaved, then slowly
calmed.  He closed
his beak, cocked his
head, and made a
quarter turn on his
perch to stare at me.
"I'm sorry," I said.
"It's glass, not sky."
The chickadee
blinked and eyed
me squarely.  "Are
you cold?" I asked.

63

"Would you like
me to hold you?"
I extended my
hand, palm stretched
flat. "Don't touch
me," he said without
words. So we sat,
the chickadee and
me, while titmice
and a nuthatch
dined at the feeder
and dry leaves
scratched their way
across the deck. Then
the bird, so small, so
delicate, crouched
like a tiger about
to pounce, and
launched himself
off the railing. He
flew to a nearby
tree where he
preened and scolded
me for living in a
house with windows.

April on the A.T.

The grouse drums;
the first startled
salamander we've
seen this season
runs and hides in
muddy water and
old leaves; the din
of peepers in the
beaver pond is
nearly deafening.

We stride in Spring
woods hoping to
renew ourselves
again, like leaves
unfurling, like pale
yellow violets, like
shoots, still curled,
and stretching
upward to the sun.

The damp ground
pulses, soft, beneath
our feet and the rain
on our faces
feels like life.

## First Leaf

The first of this year's
leaves lets go and drifts,
no breeze to bear it.
With lazy grace the leaf
unwinds its growing
season in a dancing
downward spiral, lands
in silence, making of
itself a perfect offering
to the altar of the earth.

Cathedral

I will worship
where the broad
arc of sky bends
to hear the bird song.

I will pray where
the sun's warm rays
rest on grazing sheep.

On my knees, I will gaze
in wonder at the oaks and
beeches,  hearing you in the
music of their rustling leaves.

Not one stone sanctuary
can capture the essence
or the glory that you give
so freely to the fields.

No cathedral shaped
by human hands can
hope to hold the full
measure of your mirth.

## Two Butterflies Meet

Two butterflies meet in midair.
They celebrate their intimate
pairing, and fly as one being
with mingled wings. When
their impromptu coupling is
complete, they take their leave,
no sadness in the parting.

## Beaver Pond

Things make sense here.
Trees fall when teeth
gnaw them smartly
through.  Hard work
holds the dam together.
Single tail slaps signal
danger.  Frogs croak
in bass and tenor.
Red winged blackbirds
rise from the weeds.

I need the sense I find
here; the simple, cyclic
order of season following
season, trees leafing
in the Spring to shade
Jack-in the Pulpits
pushing up through
last year's leaves.

I take my lessons
where I find them,
here where the beavers
swim in slow circles
watching me.
They wonder how I live
with such small teeth.

## Turn Your World Red

Cardinal calls me from the
railing of the deck. "Turn
your world red," he says,
insistent, beckoning. "Risk
life outside your hard-earned
walls and windows. Cast
aside caution, propriety,
and your too small sense
of what you can and cannot
do. Fly! I tell you that the
sky knows no constraints.
All you are or can be comes
clear in the near approach of
clouds. Fly! That which you
fear the most holds your
deepest teaching. Let your
spirit be the bridge between
safety and release. Soar to
the far end of what is known
from dawn to twilight, then
throw yourself at the whim
of the wild night winds.
Turn your world red, and
live with no regrets. Fly!
And if you are blown off
course, just change your
destination. Choose to
land wherever your two
feet are standing.

Born Again In Radiance

Who can resist that first,
optimistic moment of dawn –
the dazzling sliver of light,
sun rising, rounding, making
the profound shift from
promise to presence.

Every possibility contained
in a single instant; light
linking us to vastness,
light reaching back to the
formation of stars, light that
will not let us forget that we
are daily born again in radiance.

# The

# Gifts

# of

# Union

## One

Within us lie the answers
to our deepest questions
and the antidote for all
our fears.  The divine
is not an abstraction – it's
as clear and intimate as a
heartbeat or a whisper.

We are penetrated, suffused,
caressed, cell by cell and
synapse by synapse, with
the same love that set
the galaxies to spinning.

No matter how identified
we've become with mind
and body, we can release
the thoughts that blind us
to the truth.  Seek the still
point where the words "you"
and "I" lose meaning, where
we meet and merge as One.

And a voice spoke in the twilight:
"For I will carry you across the
wide river of life, and see you
safely to the other side.  Be unafraid
and joyous.  On this shared journey,
you will see miracles.  You will
know sadness.  The heart of your
heart will be glad.  And at times
you will suffer, but there won't
be a single moment when you'll
stray from the path.  If you could
only believe that right now, this
moment is part of the journey,
perhaps you'd see the futility
of worry or despair.  I will carry
you no matter if you find the way
easy and safe, or rife with danger
and impossibility.  I will keep you
in the presence of God and in the
light of truth.  This is my covenant
with you.  I speak soul to soul and
I say only what is true."  With that,
the night went back to stillness.

## Finding the Beloved

I spread the feast,
blanket bending
the slender stems
of daisies.
I cast my gaze
in all directions,
watching for my love.
I light a candle,
shelter it with
a glass chimney,
break the bread
and pour the wine,
and wait and wait,
then strain my eyes
looking to the far
horizon where the sun
sinks behind magenta
hills.  Longing fills
me, and the first star
speaks silently to me:
"The one that you await
is already within the gates;
turn your gaze inside, and
greet him."  Oh, that
meeting!  The sweet
fulfillment of the bride,
the wise stars wheeling
in the night sky…
He was with me
all the while.

## Carried to the Brink

I am aroused, awake.  I know
    the Beloved can take any form
or shape.  I watch and ache.
    The longing to behold this One
shakes me to the center of my
    soul.  I wait.  I stand at the
gates of passion, but do not
    enter in.  I am impatient.  I am
like a leaf carried downstream
    toward the falls.  Just before I
take the plunge, I am stopped
    by a branch, midstream.  I hear
the thunder, see the spray, but
    cannot embrace the destiny I
know is mine.  Oh sweep me
    free of anything that keeps me
from this One I know and long
    for.  Let me be lost in the
roaring whirl of love.  When
    the river moves to a quiet pool,
let me give all I am into the
    stillness, then take all of the
Beloved within me.  We who
    were never really two, now
drown in perfect union.

## Initiation

Oh rapturous awakening! Whirling in wide-
armed abandon, I lose myself in wind and
starlight dancing on the waves. My heart
has never tasted an embrace as deep as
this Great Lovemaking. A strong pulse
pounds in palms and feet. It bids me
laugh and weep in the same breath, then
calls me to seek the arms of the Beloved
once again. I tell you, and I know this to
be true, that I did nothing to earn this
ecstasy except say "Yes" to the tide that
waited to sweep me to the far horizon.

All I did was allow the Beloved to enter
in, to race through me like a wildfire
in the dry season, and now the very
ground I walk upon has changed.
I no longer know my name, see
nothing but the sensuous spiral of
smoke rising from the world as I
have known it. On my lips there
is the taste of salt and honey. I hear
only the wild, haunting cry of loons,
calling me to live in truth.

## Sun Kissed

The blown conch sounds
its low note.  In the warm
air, the fragrance of musk
and lilac mingle.  A wooden
flute wraps its melody around
me like silk.  The time for dry
austerities is past.  I cast my
robe aside, throw bare arms
wide and let the sunlight
have its way with me.

Curves, softness, breath, beauty,
movement, breasts seek the sun's
embrace.  A lifetime of shame
lifts, burning away like morning
mist.  Adrift, the rising tide
of passion takes me, and I
do not wish to find the shore.

# Life Here at the Edge

When love lights a fire in the heart,
don't be so quick to quell the flames.
To be fully alive is to welcome the
Beloved in countless names and guises,
not turn away the wild with the tame.

Drink your fill of longing. Let
love wash through in waves that
lift you up and carry both your
daring and your fear straight
to unknown places. Yes, there
is danger in not staying safely
cloaked in morality and labels –

But there is life here at the edge,
and a choice to be made between
thoughtful abandon and passionate
restraint. The plaintive cry of the
heart can be ignored only at the
price of a fully realized life.

Throw arms wide to possibilities
that move and call you to come
forth in freedom and in fullness.
Trust the seed of grace within to
blossom without sin or sorrow,
for you are surely big enough to
hold the truth as it unfolds.

## Metamorphosis

Called beyond the confines of this
chrysalis by a force I cannot see
or name, I am compelled by pain
and something bigger than myself
to leave the protection of all that I
have known.  There is struggle, doubt,
an awkward setting forth. Finally I
break free of the cocoon and find
myself surrounded by air and light.

I dare to act, still not knowing what
I am; instinct, or maybe faith bids me
move forward, make the leap, explore
this mystery of change and flight.

I find myself with wings that dwarf
my former world.  Unfurled, they dry
quickly in the sun.  I, who expected
 to spend my days crawling, now
teach myself to soar.  Such a rush
of wind and freedom – that  first
flight teaches me more than I had
learned in a lifetime of crawling.

## Remember This

Vast and changeless,
the ground of being
is not rocked by
ripples on the pond.

The firmament from
which we spring, the
divinity at the heart
of things doesn't wax
or wane with mind states,
or wither in the wind.

We come from stronger
stuff than feelings.
Essence does not fail
or fade, diminish or
trade reality for illusion.

We are wordless, wide,
and wise beyond time.
Within us is a flame
of truth that never dies.
Let that be the focal
point of life.  Let that
be the light that guides
us from the shadows.

Show yourself.  Here –
show yourself to me.
What use are secrets?
Stripped to your barest
essence, dancing naked
in the sun, hold nothing
back.  Would you hide
from the wild creator of
the world?  No.  Show
yourself.  Sensual, full
of grace or awkward,
base or sacred, it's all
the same to me.  I see
past skin.  Show yourself.

I hear the longing in
your morning song.
Step forward to the
sun's own spotlight.
Show yourself, and
perhaps you'll see
what I see.  Spirit,
wrapped in humanity.
Spirit, shrouded in
mystery, or shrinking
in fear.  Spirit.  You
are no different than
me.  Show yourself
and your eyes will
learn a deeper seeing.

Surrender to the
unknown.  Yes, I
hear your moans of
pleasure and delight.
Yes, that winged
spirit, that wise and

82

earthy, loving soul
taking flight; that
glowing, growing,
limited by nothing,
one with everything
radiant spirit – that is
you – that is me.
Show yourself, and
there, find freedom.

## Soul Prayer

Lord, grant that I may fall awake,
and not miss a moment of the mystery.
Dancing with the dawn, may I draw
this day to my breast like a lover.

May I, the prodigal, never lost and
ever found, feast at the table of salvation,
sipping from a shared cup, fingers lingering
together on the stem, sin such a forgotten thing.

May no false faces hide me from the
shower of your grace; mundane and sacred
cannot be distinguished in the place where
all paths lead to stillness.

Rocked with laughter, let me lay waste
the fields of doubt and fear, finding
there no more substance than dandelion
seeds flying weightless on the breeze.

Grant that I might manifest your word,
embodied essence; songs of praise
rise unbidden to my lips; held and
holding, boldly blessing, effervescent
in the merging of our souls.

## Ashes in a Sacred Fire

I am not the quiet maiden,
waiting. My longing lights
the darkness with a flame
that only you can quench.

I seek you now, in every
corner, run my trembling
hand through knotted hair,
feel the air against hot skin,
repeat, like mantra,
"Desire isn't sin."

Where are you now? The
burning in my body grows
to meet you. Take me
quickly lest the yearning
leave me dry and withered.

Let your holy fire meet
mine like lightning streaking
through the night. I would
rather be reduced to ash
in blazing consummation
than wander wide-eyed,
the promise of our union
so much smoke
upon the wind.

The seed, the spark, the very heart
      of God is present in your longing.
Look no further for fulfillment
      than the open door of your desire.
That is where divinity resides.

      Only truth can yearn for truth.

The proof of Presence lies in the
      urge to return to your own center.
Ask, and find you are the answer.
      Knock, and receive the mystery of
all that is or was or ever will be.

      Seek, and already you are found.

## Touch Me

Touch me as if you seek to find
the core of my desire.

Come to me like wind before
a summer storm.

Blown open, I close no doors
against the breeze.

Dance with me beneath the
low clouds.

Find me within you, above you,
beside you.

When the rain finally falls,
I cannot tell where you end
and I begin.

## It's Love

In the refuge of your eyes,
there can be no compromise
with truth.  The ruthless
mind may dig to find
what's lacking, but we
are the love we long for.

This outpouring of the heart,
no end, and no beginning,
bigger than our deepest fear,
fresh and clear in every moment--
it's love that makes us whole.

# True Nature

I am the bow, strung,
the arrow aimed,
the archer with
sights set on
a single mark,
the final destination
never in doubt.

I am two hands,
opened wide,
they clutch at nothing,
and instead receive
more than I could
ever think to ask for.

I am the altar,
white cloth,
spotless, spread,
the bread of life
awaits the breaking.

I am the seed,
and you the gentle
breeze that carries
me to fertile ground.

I am the blossom
and you the sun,
I the nectar, you
the broad winged
monarch, bending
to sip with such
delicate lips, the
dew of my delight.

## Lamp Light

You are the lamp, shining
in the night, and I, the
weary traveler.  I am
the hollow flute, and
you, the music.  We
weave a rich duet of
spirit; our feet fly in
a shared dance, energy
unborn and never dying.
We flow like braided
streams back to one
source.  I grow like
a tree in your orchard,
bear fruit, bend low with
laden branches.  You let
me know with each
breath the depth that
love can reach, and the
gifts that grace bestows.

Awakening, can I withstand
the radiance?  When the goddess
gazes from my eyes, when my heart
opens wide, when the current of
life sweeps me far from safety,
when even the illusion of control
is lost and what's left to me is love,
can I breathe a prayer of gratitude
and praise?  Unlike the winter
groundhog, can I raise my face
to the sun and not run from the
shadow that, embodied, I will
   always cast in daylight?

# Stardust

From a crowded firmament of
constellations, a galaxy reaches
out to stroke my cheek with a
single, spiral finger.  One star
speaks: "Life is not a test.
 There is no key to find, or
door to open.  Self-improvement
 is not the point.  There is only
awakening.  And one day you
will all awaken to the rapture
of the great lovemaking, when
the heart of everything is
revealed as you; when the myth
of separation is burned to ash
in the searing flame of truth."

A lifetime of forgetfulness
erased in an instant of
remembering. The Beloved
enters, takes me in a whirl
of tenderness and bliss.
In that moment, two are
one, and one is everything;
stars and souls are whole,
unbroken, flowing motion;
what is wrapped in skin or
cloaked in form has no birth
or death or destination.

The star speaks to me again:
"The seeds of love sown an
eternity ago are blooming now.
There has always been divinity,
and this, at last, is who we are -

love in endless consummation.
Love, not limitation, is the truth."
Then with a rush of wind like
countless wings, I am left to
sit in stillness, with the taste
of stardust sweet upon my lips.

I return to where I never
left, reconnect with that
from which I was never
separate, remember what
has always been true.

When I stop the struggle,
I expand into unbearable
awareness.

There is nothing to say,
no "You" to thank, nor
"Me" to be grateful, no
altar or supplicant, sinner
or confessional.  When
one of us sings, we all
recall the music.

# Index of Titles or First Lines

Allow, 25
And a voice spoke in the twilight, 74
April on the A.T., 65
Arriving back from the fields, 33
Ashes in a Sacred Fire, 85
Awakening, can I withstand, 91
Awakening Now, 52
Beaver Pond, 69
Being Present, 6
Birthright, 13
Black-Eyed Susans, 58
Blown conch sounds, 78
Born Again in Radiance, 71
Breaking All the Rules, 34
Breath, 4
Breath of Life, 10
Breathe, relax and feel, 6
Bull's Eye, 36
Called beyond the confines of this, 80
Cardinal calls me, 70
Carried to the Brink, 76
Cathedral, 67
Chickadee flew off the feeder, 63
Choice, 38
Despite fervent pleas for ease, 19
Despite illness of body or mind, 13
Do yoga with no goal, 5
Embodied Spirit, 41
Emerging from the darkness, 59
Enough, 30
Estuary, 61
Fear and love seldom stand, 45
Fern, furled, 60
Finding the Beloved, 75
First Leaf, 66
First of this year's leaves, 66

Foundation Stones, 26
From a crowded firmament, 92
Fruits of Practice, 19
Gifts of Life (section), 24
Gifts of Nature (section), 53
Gifts of Practice (section), 1
Gifts of Union (section), 72
Go In and In, 2
Gone Fishing, 29
Grayson Highlands, 59
Grouse drums, 65
Hands lift, float, drift, 16
Hands open to receive or give, 12
Healing, 50
Here is a day, dawn to dark, 56
Here is my past, 26
I Am All of This, 22
I am aroused, awake, 76
I am embodied, 41
I am intimately connected, 40
I am not the quiet maiden, 85
I am the bow, strung, 89
I breathe in All That Is, 10
I return to where I never left, 94
I spread the feast, 75
I tell you, this was no ordinary rainbow, 54
I will carry you across, 74
I will worship, 67
If I knew that everything I believed, 32
In the refuge of your eyes, 88
In the willingness to feel, 39
Initiation, 77
Inner Fire, 18
Is it faith or fear, 38
It Doesn't Always Smell Like Roses, 17
It only takes a reminder to breathe, 14

It's all here in this single stalk, 58
It's enough to offer love, 30
It's Love, 88
Kripalu, 21
Lamp Light, 90
Lay the Armor Down, 33
Let go of the ways you thought life, 48
Let It Go, 48
Life comes as is, no warranties, 44
Life Here At the Edge, 79
Life of truth walks the edge, 46
Life spirals in until it is a single, 47
Life will not be neatly, 37
Lord, grant that I may fall awake, 84
Loss of Innocence, 63
Meditation, 8
Metamorphosis, 80
Nothing Is Impossible, 54
Ocracoke Island, 62
Oh, rapturous awakening, 77
One, 73
Overnight, each piece of dune grass, 62
Paradox, 45
Pilgrims on the Path of Love, 47
Ragged remnants of webs, 57
Remember This, 81
Sangha, 49
Seed, the spark, the very heart, 86
Seek, and already you are found, 86
Setting Forth, 27
Show yourself, 82
Single-Celled Elegance, 55
Sit here for a bit, 3
Slow Motion Prana, 16
Something in me is being pulled, 51
Something will be born, 27

Sooner or later, life in its variety, 35
Soul of Yoga, 15
Soul Prayer, 84
Spider Webs, 57
Stardust, 92
Staring At the Bones, 35
Still Life With Fruit, 37
Still Point, 9
Successful microbes mutate, 55
Sun Kissed, 78
Surely This Is Love, 40
Teach me what I cannot learn alone, 49
There are as many paths to truth, 22
There are moments when rules, 34
There is a quality of stillness so rare, 9
There is healing in the laying on of hands, 50
There is no controlling life, 25
There is peace here, 61
Things make sense here, 69
This arrow of life, 36
This body is not flowing, 17
This is Prana, 12
This path, this place, this endeavor, 21
Together, 43
Touch, like the whisper of a wing, 8
Touch Me, 87
True Nature, 89
Turn Your World Red, 70
Two Butterflies Meet, 68
Vast and changeless, 81
Waiting for Safety, 60
Walk Slowly, 14
We call down grace, 43
Weaver and the Loom, 3
What does it take to keep the inner, 18
What is the soul of yoga, 15
When I can be the witness, 7

When I stop the struggle, 94
When love lights a fire in the heart, 79
When the sun rises in the heart, 42
Who can resist that first optimistic, 71
Who You Are, 28
Who you are is so much more, 28
Why wait for your awakening, 52
Willingness, 39
Within us lie the answers, 73
Witness, 7
Yoga, 11
Yoga is not about the pose, 11
You are the lamp, 90
You seekers of truth, 29

## Other Books by Danna Faulds

*One Soul: More Poems from the Heart of Yoga* (2003)

*Prayers to the Infinite: New Yoga Poems* (2004)

*From Root to Bloom: Yoga Poems and Other Writings* (2006)

*Limitless: New Poems and Other Writings* (2009)

*Into the Heart of Yoga: One Woman's Journey: A Memoir* (2011)

## Danna's poetry also appears in

*Sayings of Swami Kripalu: Inspiring Quotes From a Contemporary Yoga Master,* edited with commentary by Richard Faulds (2004)

*Swimming with Krishna: Teaching Stories from the Kripalu Yoga Tradition,* edited with commentary by Richard Faulds (2006)

*The Enlightenment Teachings of Yogeshwar Muni, American Disciple of Swami Kripalu,* edited by Richard Faulds (2009)

All titles are available directly from the authors by e-mailing yogapoems@aol.com. Inquire about wholesale prices for orders of five or more books. These titles are also available at Amazon.com.